EARTH'S PRECIOUS WATER

WATER QUALITY

by Helen Lepp Friesen

LIGHTBOX

Go to **www.openlightbox.com**, and enter this book's unique code.

ACCESS CODE

LBXF5466

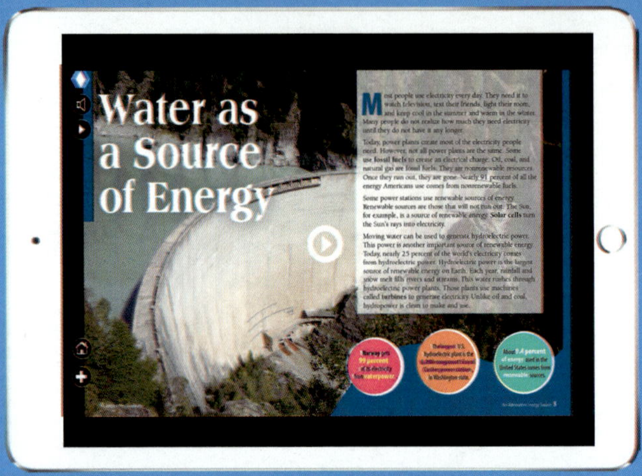

Lightbox is an all-inclusive digital solution for the teaching and learning of curriculum topics in an original, groundbreaking way. Lightbox is based on National Curriculum Standards.

STANDARD FEATURES OF LIGHTBOX

AUDIO High-quality narration using text-to-speech system

ACTIVITIES Printable PDFs that can be emailed and graded

SLIDESHOWS Pictorial overviews of key concepts

VIDEOS Embedded high-definition video clips

WEBLINKS Curated links to external, child-safe resources

TRANSPARENCIES Step-by-step layering of maps, diagrams, charts, and timelines

INTERACTIVE MAPS Interactive maps and aerial satellite imagery

QUIZZES Ten multiple choice questions that are automatically graded and emailed for teacher assessment

KEY WORDS Matching key concepts to their definitions

Contents

What is Water Pollution?

Water pollution is when **toxins** or chemicals in water harm living things or the environment. Even small amounts of these toxins or chemicals can be enough to cause serious damage. Lakes, seas, creeks, rivers, and other large bodies of water can all become polluted.

There are different sources of water pollution. Infectious substances found in **sewage**, such as bacteria, viruses, and parasites, can cause water pollution. Radioactive waste has large amounts of uranium and radon. Mining companies and power plants can pollute water with their waste.

Many different chemicals can **contaminate** water. They can be found in nature, such as many acids, salts, or metals. They may also be human-made, such as chemicals in **pesticides**, plastics, detergents, or oil. Fertilizers from farming activity can pollute **groundwater**.

People can become exposed to water pollution in different ways. They may drink water that is polluted, swim or wash in contaminated water, breath fumes from a polluted water source, or eat food that has been contaminated with water pollution.

Water pollution can have different effects on people. It can cause diseases and health threats. Symptoms may appear right after being exposed or years later. The effects of exposure to contaminated water can range from mild to severe. It depends how contaminated the water is and how intense and long the exposure is.

Unsafe drinking water systems affect **18 million** Americans.

In the **United States**, there are more than **5,000 water systems** that **do not comply** with **safe drinking water laws**.

About **300,000 gallons** (1.1 million liters) of **sewage** was **dumped** in **Boca Ciega Bay, Florida**, in late summer of 2016.

Pollution in the Ocean

About 70 percent of Earth is made of water. Most of this is in the oceans. These water sources are very important for humans to survive. However, human activity can harm marine environments. The dumping of garbage and waste is the primary cause of pollution in the ocean. Dumping includes waste from factories, ships, cities, and towns. Waste causes oxygen in the ocean to decrease, harming sea life.

The Pacific Garbage Patch, also called the Pacific trash **vortex**, is located in the northern Pacific Ocean. It is the biggest pool of marine waste on Earth, covering the waters from the west coast of North America all the way to Japan. Much of the debris is plastic. About 70 percent of this waste drops to the bottom of the ocean.

Other forms of ocean pollution include oil spills. These can happen during oil well drilling, repairs, or transportation. When oil spills in water, it first covers the water's surface. Wind and water currents spread the oil over the water. The explosive parts of the oil **evaporate**, losing about 20 to 40 percent of the oil mass. Then, the mass becomes thick and sticky. Oil washes up on the shoreline. The **oil slick** is harmful to both animals and plants. Long-term effects of an oil spill can be very damaging. Entire food chains may be destroyed.

About 30,000 birds were killed as a result of the Gulf War oil spill.

Fish eggs and young were covered with oil. This reduced the breeding of some bird species that relied on them for food by 50 percent in the year after the oil spill.

About one million barrels worth of oil were recovered from the Gulf.

The Largest Oil Spill on Record

When: 1991 | **Where:** Kuwait

The largest oil spill in history took place during the Gulf War. Retreating soldiers from Iraq destroyed tankers, storage tanks, and port facilities, dumping oil into the Persian Gulf. Ultimately, about 240 million gallons of oil were dumped into the ocean near Kuwait and Saudi Arabia. By the time the cleanup started, much of the oil had already sunk.

DISCUSSION

What can be done to prevent oil spills? Explain how your suggestions can be implemented.

The oil spill caused about $540 million dollars in damages.

Scientists were not able to access the site to help with recovery efforts until the war had ended.

By 2010, the area had nearly fully recovered.

Industrial pollution makes up more than half of the total pollution in the United States.

Industrial Pollution

Industry and agriculture are major sources of water pollution. Many industries dispose of their waste into freshwater that feeds into rivers, lakes, and oceans. Polluted water is not suitable for drinking or for irrigating crops. It affects humans, animals, and plants. Pollution can enter the water in other ways. Some farms burn crop waste. Burning crop waste puts fumes, including ammonia, nitrogen oxide, methane, and carbon monoxide into the air. Farm machinery, such as tractors, may run on petroleum. Pollution goes into the air from the exhaust. All of these forms of aerial pollution can become part of rain or snow as it falls to the ground.

Lead is a metal that occurs naturally in the soil. When it is used to make batteries, paint, and metal products, it can enter into the water. When lead leaches into drinking water, humans can be affected. Lead poisoning can cause brain, stomach, and kidney damage. Over time, lead exposure can affect the nervous system, cause high blood pressure, and lead to other serious health issues. Long-term lead exposure can be fatal.

The Industrial Revolution of the mid 19th century brought many advances in technology. It also introduced new and dangerous sources of air and water pollution. In the mid-20th century, the effects of the Industrial Revolution were felt all around the world. On June 22, 1969, the Cuyahoga River in Cleveland, Ohio, burst into flames. A spark from a passing train ignited oil-soaked garbage floating in the river. Although it was not the first fire or the worst, this particular incident caused nation-wide concern. It became the reason for an amendment to the Federal Water Pollution Control Act of 1948. After the amendment was passed, the act was renamed the Clean Water Act. These changes set new clean water standards and added new rules about who could dump chemicals into the water.

About half of oil pipelines in the United States are more than 50 years old. This increases the chances of leaks as they weaken over time.

The **Federal Water Pollution Control Act** was the **first major** U.S. law relating to water pollution.

The **1969 Cuyahoga River fire caused $50,000** in damages.

There has **not been a fire** on the **Cuyahoga River** since 1969.

Pollution at Home

Studies have shown that pesticides can leach into the groundwater below. Groundwater is used as drinking water by more than 50 percent of Americans.

Household products can contribute to polluting the environment. Common household pollutants include cleaning supplies, paints, lawn and garden care products, car products, chemicals for pools, and health and beauty aids. Today, more environmentally-friendly products are being put on the market. These "green" products do not put a heavy burden on the environment when they are made, used, and disposed of.

Lawn care products, such as pesticides, weed killers, and fertilizers, are used for maintaining lawns. Toxins in these products may become airborne, eventually entering the water as precipitation. They may also be tracked indoors on shoes, toys, or pets, making their way into the water system when the object or animal is washed. When lawns are watered, these chemicals may be washed into drains.

COMMON HARMFUL HOUSEHOLD PRODUCTS AND "GREEN" ALTERNATIVES

Product Type	Harmful Ingredient	Health Hazard	Alternative
Air freshener	Formaldehyde	Irritates eyes, nose, throat, and skin	Natural scents such as cinnamon, vanilla, or herbs, open windows
Toilet bowl cleaner	Hypochloric acid	Toxic, burns skin	Baking soda or vinegar
Furniture polish	Petroleum-based product	Flammable, enters water system, burns skin, toxic	Mixture of lemon and mineral oil
Laundry detergent	Phosphates	Irritates skin, can cause cancer	Biodegradable laundry detergent
Paint	Oil-based product, mineral spirits	Flammable, irritates skin	Water-based paint
Oven Cleaner	Lye	Toxic, burns skin, enters the water stream	Baking Soda

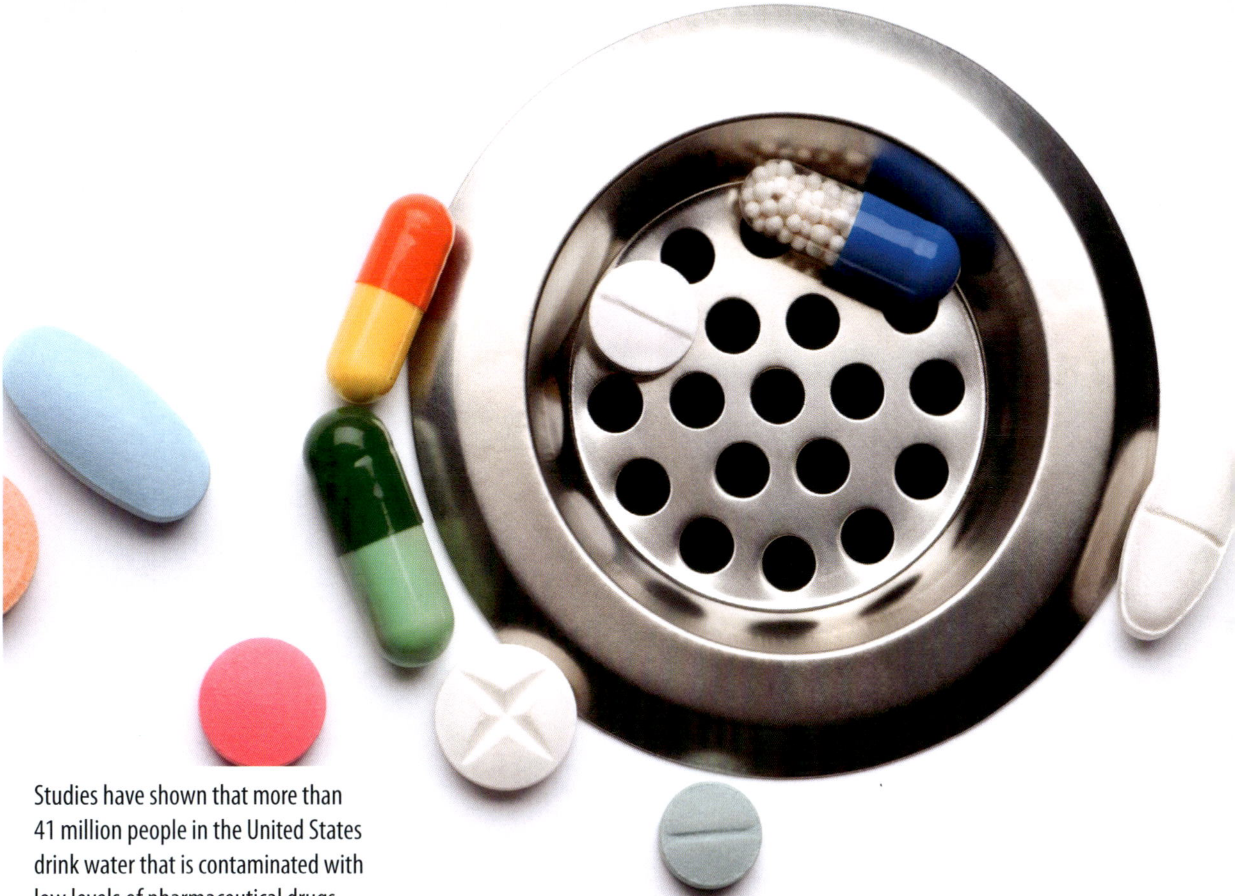

Studies have shown that more than 41 million people in the United States drink water that is contaminated with low levels of pharmaceutical drugs.

Remainders from pills, shampoos, and prescription drugs can also enter the water supply. Even though medications are ingested, the chemicals make their way through the digestive system and into drains. They are eventually flushed into the water system. Some people wash expired or unused drugs down the drain or flush them. Pharmacies and hospitals are setting up locations where people can bring their expired drugs for proper disposal.

More Americans are living longer and using more medications. This means that more chemicals are introduced into the water stream. Chemicals and hormones in the water are affecting fish and marine life. They can affect the way these animals grow and mature. Today, scientists study the risk of these substances to both humans and the environment.

Drinking Water Quality

Safe drinking water is essential to health. Water quality is measured to see if it meets safe guidelines. Water is tested for mineral content, metals, and other things that could be dangerous to human health. Governments and agencies have developed rules for safe water to protect people. The United States passed the Safe Drinking Water Act in 1974 to protect the nation's drinking water supplies.

In the United States, water systems serve millions of people. Water is piped to homes in 99 percent of the United States. Although most people do have access to safe, clean water in the United States, there are many water quality problems as well. These issues occur most often in more isolated locations, such as in small rural communities.

In many American cities, drinking water is tested hourly to make sure it is safe to drink. The Environmental Protection Agency (EPA) requires testing for more than 90 different contaminants in public drinking water.

People living in poorer communities are also more likely to be exposed to poor water quality. Many problems with water quality have occurred in areas where residents live below the poverty line. Corpus Christi, Texas, has had many water problems in the past decade. In 2016, chemicals from a local industry leaked into the water. People were not able to use the water for almost four days. Today, activists and journalists are studying environmental fairness when it comes to safe drinking water.

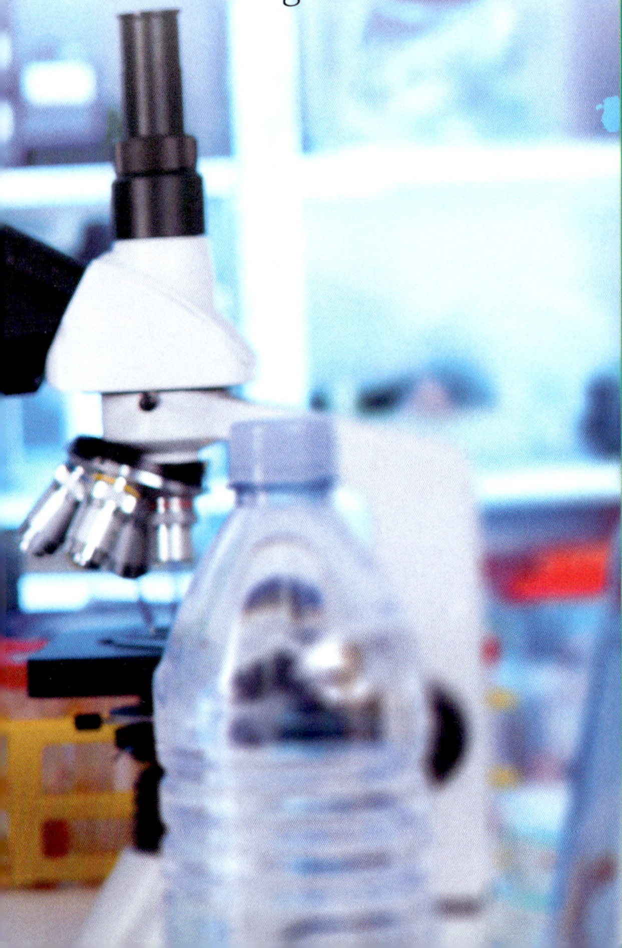

Flint Water Crisis

In 2011, the city of Flint, Michigan, was building a new pipeline. It would bring water from Lake Huron to Flint. During construction, Flint used the Flint River as their source of water. Soon, residents noticed that the water looked, smelled, and tasted odd. In 2015, the EPA tested the water. It had dangerous levels of lead. About half of the water lines to homes were made of lead. The water was not properly treated, causing lead to leach into it. Many lawsuits were filed against the city and its managers.

Flint Water Crisis Key Dates

March 22, 2012: Announcement of construction of the new pipeline to deliver water from Lake Huron to Flint.

April 25, 2014: Flint switches its water source to Flint River.

August 14, 2014: A boil water advisory is prompted due to unhealthy bacteria in the water.

January 21, 2015: Residents bring jugs of brown water to a community meeting. Children throughout the city are suffering from rashes and illnesses.

February 26, 2015: The EPA detects dangerous levels of lead in the water.

December 14, 2015: Flint declares a state of emergency.

January 12, 2016: The National Guard helps distribute bottled water.

February 17, 2017: The Michigan Civil Rights Commission indicates that decisions leading to the crisis were made because of discriminatory reasons.

April 6, 2018: The free bottled water program ends.

Acid Rain

Acid rain is when rain, snow, or fog falling to the ground has high levels of nitric and sulfuric acids. Erupting volcanoes or rotting plants naturally release some chemicals that cause acid rain. However, human activity is responsible for most acid rain. Cars, factories, and coal-burning plants all contribute to produce acid rain. It is created when humans burn fossil fuels. This releases chemicals known as sulfur dioxide and nitrogen oxide into the air. When these chemicals react with water, oxygen, and other particles in the air, they produce nitric and sulfuric acid. Wind carries the acidic solution. When acid rain falls to the ground, it enters the water system and soil.

In North America, 30 percent of acid rain comes from motor vehicle emissions. These emissions also create smog that makes it difficult to see things that are far away.

A major effect of acid rain falls on **aquatic environments**, such as lakes and rivers. Acid rain makes water acidic. This causes water to absorb aluminum that washes into lakes and rivers. Chemicals and aluminum in the water harm marine plants and animals. Eventually, this pollution can also affect other species that do not live in water when they eat contaminated marine life. Acid rain also damages forests. It takes away essential nutrients from the soil when it is absorbed into the ground. It can make it harder for trees to absorb water and nutrients. Trees become less able to tolerate extreme temperatures, insects, and diseases.

Trees that have been weakened by acid rain are more vulnerable to wood-eating insects.

In the 1980s, the towering red spruce, in New England, began to show the effects of acid rain. Some trees were taller than eight-story buildings. However, these trees began to look sickly and many died. Other trees were also affected. Sugar maples, balsam fir, and beech trees all showed signs of ill health. In response to the environmental crisis, Congress added the Acid Rain Program to the Clean Air Act in 1990. Between 1995 and 2011, air quality improved. Studies show that today, the red spruce trees are regaining their health.

In the **1980s**, scientists **tried to neutralize acid** in New York's Wolf Pond **by pouring 14 tons** (12.7 metric tons) of **baking soda** into it.

Acid rain has the **same level of acidity** as **orange juice** and **vinegar**.

In the United States, **electric power generation** is responsible for about **69 percent** of **sulfur dioxide emissions.**

Urban Planners

An urban planner is someone who makes plans for a city or community. The goal of an urban planner is to make sure that the community functions well. They are responsible for many different tasks. Transportation, environmental issues, and urban design for a community are all part of their job. Some urban planners help plan parks. They may analyze traffic trends and plan affordable housing. They make sure sewer and water services are adequate.

Water Pollution History

1989

The cleanup after the Exxon Valdez oil spill, off the coast of Alaska, requires the help of many government and state officials. Efforts and plans are made to prevent such an accident from occurring again.

1917

The American City Planning Institute is founded. Its members are leaders that plan healthy communities. It was later renamed the American Planning Association.

1972

The Federal Water Pollution Control Act is amended, becoming the Clean Water Act. The Clean Water Act sets standards for water use, which are used today by urban planners.

Most urban planners have a master's degree in urban and regional planning. Since they work with many other people, it is important that they have good problem solving and communication skills. Usually, urban planners work for cities or state governments. Urban planners work with teams. These may include engineers, architects, and real estate developers.

The American Planning Association (APA) is a professional organization that provides leadership in developing and planning healthy communities. The APA was originally called the American City Planning Institute. In October 1978 it was renamed. Today, it has about 38,000 members.

2002

Bangkok, Thailand experiences urban flooding due to extreme rainfall. The city's drains are not designed to manage this overload of water.

2016

During the Flint Water Crisis, investigations take place into decisions made by urban planners about water quality that impacted thousands of people.

2017

Urban flooding continues to be a major issue in developing countries. Urban development and flood management is very important in locations such as the Andalien River basin, in Chile, which has experienced 21 floods in the past 50 years.

Water Pollution around the World

1 Bligh Reef, United States

On March 24, 1989 the Exxon Valdez tanker ran aground on Bligh Reef. The accident spilled 11 million gallons (41 million L) of oil into Prince William Sound, in the Gulf of Alaska. About 1,300 miles (2,092 km) of shoreline is affected. At the time, it was the largest oil spill in U.S. history.

2 Three Mile Island, United States

On March 28, 1979, the Three Mile Island nuclear power plant near Harrisburg, Pennsylvania, broke down. Plant life and water had to be cleaned, and thousands of samples were taken to ensure that the nearby area was not affected. In the aftermath of the event, many other nuclear power plants in the United States were closed.

3 Sian Ka'an , Mexico

Sian Ka'an is a biosphere reserve and World Heritage site on the eastern coast of the Yucatán peninsula in Mexico. In the Mayan language, *Sian Ka'an* means "origin of the sky." To raise awareness and to educate about the need to protect areas such as Sian Ka'an, artist Alejandro Durán collects trash that washes up on the beach and uses it to make art. He has found products from 53 different countries.

4 Bhopal, India

On December 3, 1984, about 45 tons (41 metric tons) of a dangerous gas leaked from an American insecticide plant in the city of Bhopal. About 20,000 people died, and millions more suffered from eye and lung problems. The gas made its way into the water and soil. Today, contaminated water and soil still cause health problems in the area.

5 Ōkuma, Japan

The Fukushima Nuclear Accident at the Fukushima Daiichi nuclear power plant in northern Japan was the second-worst nuclear power plant accident in history. On March 11, 2011 an earthquake sent tsunami waves onto Japan. This damaged the backup generators of the Fukushima Daiichi plant. The accident released radioactive water into the Pacific Ocean. The cleanup from the accident continues today.

6 Great Barrier Reef, Australia

Acid rain is affecting the world's coral reefs. Burning fossil fuels emit carbon dioxide. Oceans absorb about 33 percent of the carbon dioxide from the atmosphere. This causes ocean water to become too acidic for coral to survive. Australia's Great Barrier Reef, the world's largest living structure, is at risk.

Water Quality Management

People, organizations, and governments can do things to ensure good water quality. Using research online and in the library, find out how people have dealt with incidents or accidents that have affected the quality of water near you.

WHAT HAPPENED?

Choose an incident that impacted the quality of water in your area. Where did it take place? Was the disaster caused by nature or by humans? Could it happen again?

WHAT ARE THE EFFECTS?

Find out how this incident affected your area. How much damage did it cause? Were any people harmed by it? Were there safety measures in place to stop it? Did they work?

WHAT CAN BE DONE?

Research what happened after the event. How did repairs take place? Were any steps taken to make sure that it would not happen again? Were any steps taken to prepare if it did happen again? Are there any steps that could have been taken but were not? If so, why?

Clean Water Activity

Materials

sand

two glass jars

plastic strainer

coffee filter

alum

Instructions

Step 1: Collect a water sample from a pond or puddle nearby. Put the water in two glass jars. Set one jar aside for later comparison.

Step 2: Add two teaspoons of alum to the water sample. Shake. Let it sit for a few hours. Note any changes.

Step 3: Put sand into a plastic container that has holes on the bottom. Pour the pond water through the sand. Catch the filtered water. Note the changes.

Step 4: Pour the filtered water through a coffee filter to catch any other small pieces of dirt. Note the changes.

Step 5: Compare the two jars of water.

Quiz

Test your knowledge by answering these questions. All of the information can be found in the text you just read. The answers are provided below for easy reference.

1. Into what body of water did the Exxon Valdez spill 11 million gallons of crude oil?

2. What is the Pacific Garbage Patch?

3. What is the name of the artist who collects beach trash and makes art with it?

4. What did scientists pour into Wolf Pond in New York to neutralize the acidity?

5. What event in the 19th century brought new technology and dangerous environmental impacts?

6. Can oil spills harm plants?

7. What is acid rain as acidic as?

8. Where is the Great Barrier Reef?

9. In North America, what percent of acid rain comes from vehicles?

10. What is the name of the nuclear power plant that broke down in Pennsylvania?

ANSWER KEY

1. Prince William Sound, Gulf of Alaska **2.** The biggest collection of marine waste **3.** Alejandro Durán **4.** Baking soda **5.** The Industrial Revolution **6.** Yes **7.** Orange juice and vinegar **8.** Australia **9.** 30 **10.** Three Mile Island

Key Words

acid rain: rain, snow, or fog falling that has high levels of nitric and sulfuric acids

aquatic environments: places in or near water where plants and animals live

contaminate: causing something to be polluted by a poisonous substance

evaporate: turn from liquid into vapor

groundwater: water stored in the soil

oil slick: a layer of oil floating on the water's surface

pesticides: substances that get rid of insects that are harmful to plants

sewage: waste water that includes human urine and solid waste

toxins: poisonous substances in the water, soil, or air that cause disease in people or harms the environment

vortex: a mass of whirling fluid

Index

LIGHTBOX

SUPPLEMENTARY RESOURCES

Click on the plus icon found in the bottom left corner of each spread to open additional teacher resources.

- Download and print the book's quizzes and activities
- Access curriculum correlations
- Explore additional web applications that enhance the Lightbox experience

LIGHTBOX DIGITAL TITLES
Packed full of integrated media

VIDEOS

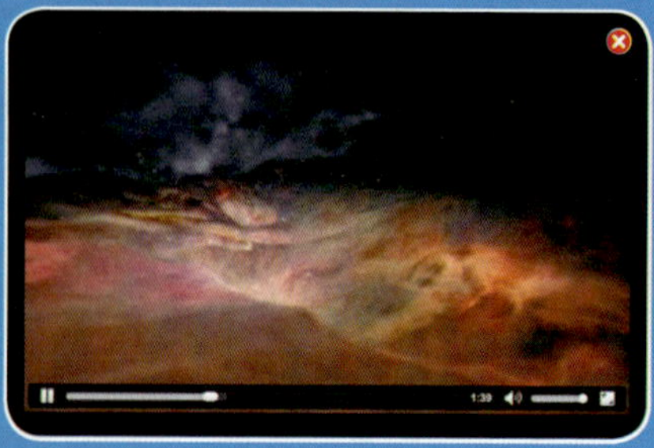

INTERACTIVE MAPS

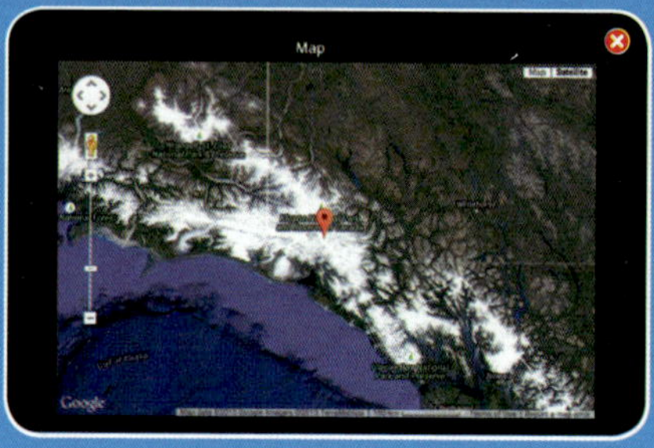

WEBLINKS

SLIDESHOWS

QUIZZES

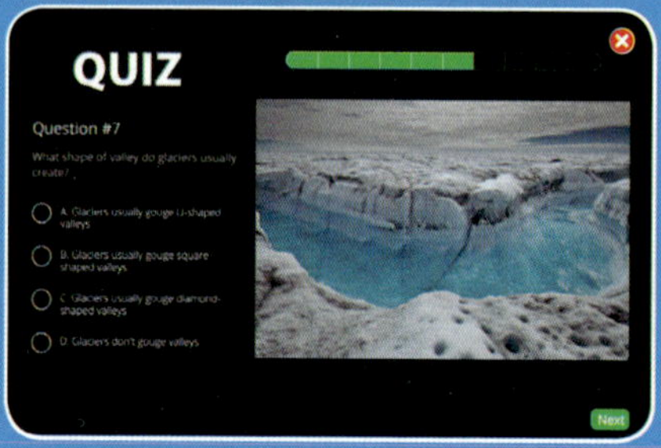

OPTIMIZED FOR
- ✓ TABLETS
- ✓ WHITEBOARDS
- ✓ COMPUTERS
- ✓ AND MUCH MORE!

Published by Smartbook Media Inc.
350 5th Avenue, 59th Floor
New York, NY 10118
Website: www.openlightbox.com

Library of Congress Control Number: 2018944576

ISBN 978-1-5105-3891-7 (hardcover)
ISBN 978-1-5105-3892-4 (multi-user eBook)

Printed in Brainerd, Minnesota, United States
1 2 3 4 5 6 7 8 9 0 22 21 20 19 18

072018
120517

Project Coordinator John Willis
Art Director Terry Paulhus

Photo Credits
Every reasonable effort has been made to trace ownership and to obtain permission to reprint copyright material. The publisher would be pleased to have any errors or omissions brought to its attention so that they may be corrected in subsequent printings. The publisher acknowledges Alamy, Getty Images, iStock, Newscom, and Shutterstock as its primary image suppliers for this title.